Parasaurolophus

by Daniel Cohen

Consultant:
Larry Dean Martin, Ph.D.
Professor-Senior Curator
Natural History Museum and Biodiversity Research Center
University of Kansas, Lawrence, Kansas

Bridgestone Books
an imprint of Capstone Press
Mankato, Minnesota

Bridgestone Books are published by Capstone Press
151 Good Counsel Drive, P.O. Box 669, Mankato, Minnesota 56002
http://www.capstonepress.com

Library of Congress Cataloging-in-Publication Data
Cohen, Daniel, 1936–
    Parasaurolophus / by Daniel Cohen.
        p. cm.—(Discovering dinosaurs)
    Summary: Introduces what is known of the physical characteristics, behavior, and habitat of
this crested dinosaur.
    Includes bibliographical references and index.
    ISBN 0-7368-2524-X (hardcover)
    1. Parasaurolophus—Juvenile literature. [1. Parasaurolophus. 2. Dinosaurs.] I. Title.
QE862.O65C623 2004
567.914—dc22   2003012377

Editorial Credits
Amanda Doering, editor; Linda Clavel, series designer; Enoch Peterson, cover production
    designer and illustrator; Alta Schaffer, photo researcher; Karen Risch, product planning editor

Photo Credits
Chase Studio/Photo Researchers, 4
Corbis/Kevin Schafer, 18
Francois Gohier, cover, 1, 10; Photo Researchers, 12
Nicholas Dollack, 16
Rich Penney, www.dinosaur-man.com, 6
The Natural History Museum/Orbis, 8, 14

1 2 3 4 5 6 09 08 07 06 05 04

Table of Contents

Parasaurolophus compared to a
5-foot-tall (1.5-meter-tall) human

4

Parasaurolophus

Parasaurolophus was a large **dinosaur** that ate plants. An adult parasaurolophus (PAR-ah-SORE-OL-o-fus) was 33 feet (10 meters) long. It weighed about 4 tons (3.6 metric tons). Saurolophus means "crested lizard." Parasaurolophus had a long, bony crest on the top of its head.

crest
a bony plate on the top of a dinosaur's head

The World of Parasaurolophus

Parasaurolophus lived in what is now western North America. It lived 75 million years ago. Earth was different then. The climate was warmer and wetter than it is now.

climate
the usual weather in a place

Maiasaura

8

Relatives of Parasaurolophus

Parasaurolophus belonged to a group of dinosaurs called hadrosaurs (HAD-roh-SORES). This group was also called "duck-billed" dinosaurs because of their bony beaks. Maiasaura (my-ah-SORE-ah) was a relative of parasaurolophus.

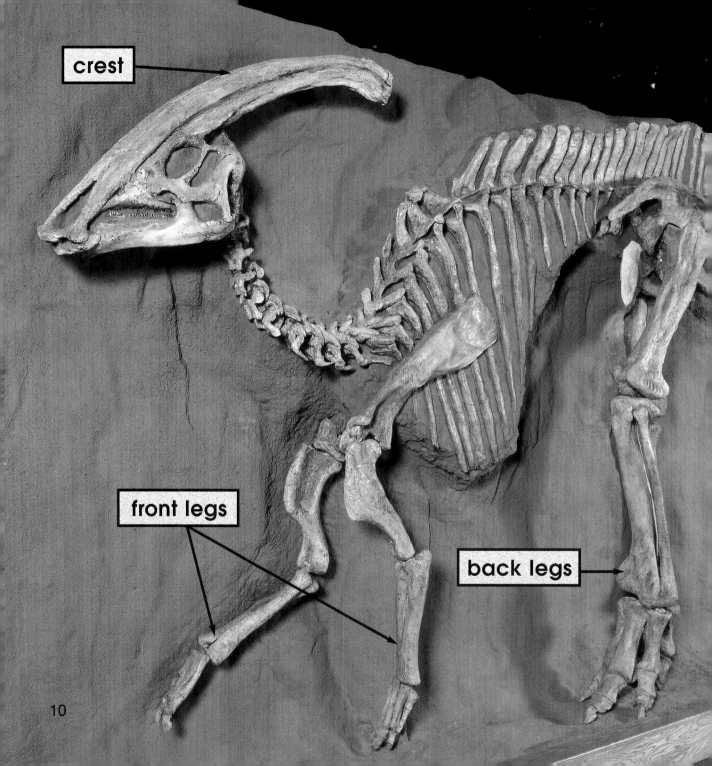

crest

front legs

back legs

Parts of Parasaurolophus

Parasaurolophus had large, strong back legs. Its front legs were shorter and smaller. Parasaurolophus used its thick tail for **balance**. A hollow, tube-shaped crest curved back from its snout. The crest was up to 6 feet (1.8 meters) long.

hollow
having an empty space

Crested Dinosaur

Scientists think parasaurolophus made sounds with its crest. It forced air through its crest to make a honking noise. This sound may have warned other dinosaurs of danger. The sound also may have attracted a mate.

mate
the male or female partner in a pair of animals

What Parasaurolophus Ate

Parasaurolophus was a **herbivore**. It ate plants. The dinosaur tore leaves off trees with its bony beak. It ground plants and twigs with its rows of flat teeth.

Predators

Parasaurolophus had several predators. A large meat-eating dinosaur like albertosaurus (al-BURT-oh-SORE-us) may have hunted parasaurolophus by itself. Smaller meat-eaters like dromaeosaurus (drom-AY-oh-SORE-us) may have hunted parasaurolophus in packs.

predator
an animal that hunts other animals for food

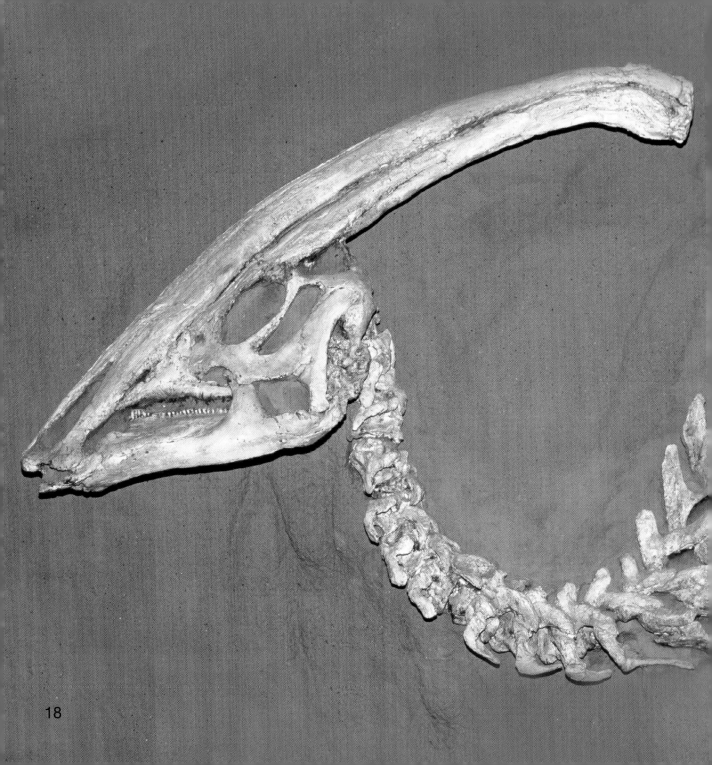

End of Parasaurolophus

Parasaurolophus lived until 65 million years ago. At that time, all dinosaurs became **extinct**. No one is sure what happened. Some scientists think a large meteorite from space struck Earth. Effects from this meteorite may have killed the dinosaurs.

meteorite

a rock that falls from space to Earth

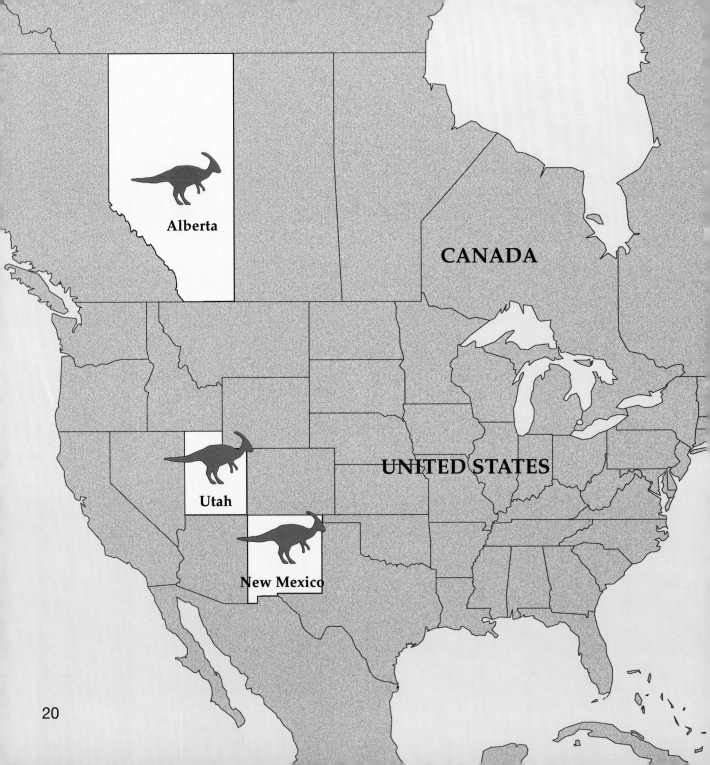

Alberta

CANADA

Utah

UNITED STATES

New Mexico

Discovering Parasaurolophus

In 1922, Dr. William A. Parks discovered a dinosaur skeleton in Alberta, Canada. The skeleton had almost all of its bones. Parks named the new dinosaur parasaurolophus. People found other parasaurolophus **fossils** in the U.S. states of New Mexico and Utah.

Hands On: Parasaurolophus Sounds

Parasaurolophus made deep, foghorn like sounds. The length of its crest determined how low the sounds were. Make your own horns to see how length affects sound.

What You Need

3 sheets of construction paper
Toilet paper tube
Tape
Paper towel tube
Wrapping paper tube

What You Do

1. With one sheet of construction paper, make a funnel shape around the end of the toilet paper tube.
2. Tape the funnel around the end of the toilet paper tube. Make sure no air is leaking between the funnel and the tube.
3. Practice buzzing your lips. Keep your mouth closed but try to blow air through your lips to make them vibrate.
4. When you are able to buzz your lips, put the horn to your mouth. Buzz your lips through the horn. How does it sound?
5. Repeat steps 1–4 with the paper towel tube and the wrapping paper tube. What happens to the sound as the tube gets longer? Which horn makes the lowest sound?

Glossary

balance (BAL-uhnss)—ability to keep steady without falling

dinosaur (DYE-na-sore)—an extinct land reptile; dinosaurs lived on Earth at least 150 million years.

extinct (EK-stingkt)—no longer living anywhere in the world

fossil (FOSS-uhl)—the remains of something that was once alive; bones and footprints can be fossils.

herbivore (HUR-buh-vor)—an animal that eats only plants

scientist (SYE-uhn-tist)—a person who studies the world around us

Read More

Barrett, Paul M. *National Geographic Dinosaurs.* Washington D.C.: National Geographic Society, 2001.

White, David. *Parasaurolophus.* Dinosaur Library. Vero Beach, Fla.: Rourke, 2001.

Internet Sites

FactHound offers a safe, fun way to find Internet sites related to this book. All of the sites on FactHound have been researched by our staff.

Here's how:
1. Visit *www.facthound.com*
2. Type in this special code **073682524X** for age-appropriate sites. Or enter a search word related to this book for a more general search.
3. Click on the Fetch It button.

FactHound will fetch the best sites for you!

Index